NO RC 9-26-16

HUNTERS GLEN LMC
13222 CORONA ST.
THORNTON, CO 80241

CATTLE

CATTLE

understanding
ANIMALS

By
Dorothy
Hinshaw
Patent

photographs
by
William
Muñoz

Carolrhoda Books, Inc.
Minneapolis

The author and photographer would like to thank the following people for their help with this book: John Bender, Keith Cable, Nancy Deschamps, H. Corwin Hinshaw, Jean Melton, Ray "Pat" Miller, John Muñoz, Steve and Maria Nelson, Larry Richards, Jerry Roselip, George Ruffatto, Gary Simonson, Jane Sparr, and Cindy and Buddy Westphal. We also want to thank Fossil Rim Wildlife Park, the National Bison Range, the Ravalli County Fair, San Diego Zoological Garden, San Diego Wild Animal Park, and Yellowstone National Park.

For Ruth

Additional photographs courtesy of: pp. 8 (top), 14 (left), 16, 17, 26, 27, Dorothy Hinshaw Patent; p. 20 (left), H. Corwin Hinshaw

Words that appear in **bold** type are listed in the glossary on page 47.

Ruth Berman, Series Editor
Zachary Marell, Series Designer

Library of Congress Cataloging-in-Publication Data

Patent, Dorothy Hinshaw.
    Cattle / by Dorothy Hinshaw Patent ; photographs by William Muñoz.
        p.   cm.
    Includes index.
    Summary: Describes the physical characteristics and behavior of cattle around the world and their evolution from their ancestors, aurochsen, which have been extinct since 1627.
    ISBN 0-87614-765-1
    1. Cattle—Juvenile literature. 2. Bovidae—Juvenile literature.
[1. Cattle. 2. Bovidae.] I. Muñoz, William, ill. II. Title.
SF197.5.P36 1993
636.2—dc20
                                                              92-32987
                                                                 CIP
                                                                  AC

Manufactured in the United States of America

1   2   3   4   5   6   98   97   96   95   94   93

Contents

Chapter 1

Where Cattle Come From

These cattle (opposite and above) are familiar to us.

For thousands of years, cattle have helped humankind, providing food and other important products. In fact, we have found more uses for cattle than for any other domesticated animal. While cattle are alive, their manure can be used for fertilizer and for fuel. They are strong enough to pull plows and carts, and they produce abundant milk that can be made into products like yogurt, butter, and cheese. When one is killed, just about every part of its body can be used. Such a large animal provides a lot of meat. The hide makes tough, durable leather, and the bones and horns can be turned into weapons and tools. The hooves provide glue and gelatin, and the fat can be burned for light and heat.

KINDS OF CATTLE

Two basic types of domesticated cattle exist. *Bos taurus* is the most familiar to us. The breeds of cattle we usually see are varieties of this species, and they all have ears that stand upright. The other type, the zebu, is given a different name by some scientists—*Bos indicus*. These cattle have drooping ears, a hump on their shoulders, and a dewlap under their chin and neck. The Brahman bulls used in rodeos are zebus. Zebus are also the sacred cattle of India and are found in other parts of Asia and Africa. They are especially resistant to insects, ticks, and heat. Zebus mate easily with other cattle and are used in breeding cattle that will do well in hot, humid areas. The Santa Gertrudis and Brangus breeds, developed in the United States, are part zebu.

Cattle belong to a large scientific family called the Bovidae. Members of this family, called bovids, include not only cattlelike animals such as bison and water buffalo but also goats, sheep, and many types of antelope. There are 128 different species of bovids living in Africa, Europe, Asia, and North America. All these animals share a trait that helps explain why they are so widespread; they have a digestive system that allows them to feed rapidly, filling their stomachs with barely chewed food. Later, they chew their food more thoroughly while they are resting. Bovids are **ruminants**, a term derived from the word *rumen*, the name for the first chamber of their four-chambered stomachs.

HOW RUMINANTS FEED

Ruminants can feed on plants like tough, dry grasses that would seem to have little food value. The tough material, called **cellulose**, that makes up most of the volume of plant leaves and stems is difficult to digest. But ruminants can digest cellulose, although they do it in a roundabout way. A

Left: *Blue wildebeest are members of the bovid family.*

Below: *Digestion begins when food enters the rumen (1) and reticulum (2). Muscles in the reticulum push the food back up where it is rechewed as cud. The cud then passes through the rumen and reticulum to the omasum (3) and abomasum (4), where digestion is completed.*

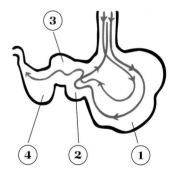

Opposite (top): *The animal at right is a Brahman cross.*

Opposite (bottom): *These cattle living in Texas are Brahman crosses.*

Cattle can get nourishment from food like hay because bacteria in their stomachs can digest cellulose.

ruminant's stomach teems with countless bacteria and one-celled creatures called protozoans. These microscopic living things do the actual digesting of the cellulose. Some of the bacteria turn the food into protein and vitamins that ruminants need to stay healthy. Without the bacteria and protozoans living in their stomachs, ruminants would starve to death no matter how much they ate.

A ruminant's long tongue twists around the food, which is then cut off by the lower front teeth biting against a tough pad on the upper jaw (ruminants don't have upper front teeth). Digestion begins when the food passes into the rumen, then to the second stomach chamber. After feeding, the ruminant lies down and rests, often in the shade during the hot part of the day. It brings the food it swallowed back up into its mouth and chews it thoroughly; this is called chewing the cud. The food is swallowed again and stays in the first two stomach chambers for several days. Eventually, it passes into the last two chambers, where digestion is completed. The special way ruminants digest their food produces lots of gas, so they belch often.

BEING A BOVID

Bovids share other traits besides their way of feeding. The males always have horns. The females of most species have horns as well, although they are often smaller and shaped differently from those of the males. Almost all bovids live in groups, often in vast herds as do the wildebeest of Africa and the bison that once roamed the plains of North America.

Below: *Bovids have an evolutionary advantage because they can eat quickly, then chew their food later in a protected place if necessary, thus avoiding predators.*

Left: *The male bluebuck, a bovid, has spectacular horns.*

Females and their young live together, while males may stay together in all-male groups or live separately as lone bulls.

The words used to describe bovids can be confusing. People often use the word *cow* to mean any individual of *Bos taurus*, the scientific name for domesticated cattle. But the word *cow* should be used only for females, while males are called bulls. There is no word to describe just one individual of *Bos taurus* without indicating its gender. Although all bovid females are called cows and all males are called bulls, most species do have a singular name—you can point and say, "That's a bison," or "That's a yak."

Most bovids are territorial—that is, the males defend a particular area where they live. But cattle and their closest relatives are not territorial. This is part of what made them easy to **domesticate**. They weren't attached to one particular place, and the bulls didn't need to fight to claim ground.

Cattle standing in a pasture, quietly feeding on grass or hay, look totally tame. It's hard to believe that they were ever wild. But the wild ancestors of cattle were quite fierce. How did people manage to domesticate them? Where did these wonderfully useful animals come from?

The young males, females, and calves of bovids like these bison live together.

Left: *Cattle today are represented by a variety of breeds and colors.*

THE GIANT AUROCHS

The ancestor of cattle, called the aurochs (plural aurochsen), has been **extinct** since 1627. That makes it difficult to know just what changes cattle underwent as they were first **tamed**, then domesticated. We do, at least, have a good idea what aurochsen looked like. They were much bigger than modern cattle. Aurochs bulls stood as tall as 6.5 feet at the shoulder, and their horns could be 3 feet long. Cattle today are rarely taller than 4 feet at the shoulder, and the horns of most are quite short. Some breeds never grow horns at all.

The aurochsen's necks and shoulders were heavily muscled, while their hindquarters were slender. They had rather long legs, straight backs, and narrow heads. Their fur was smooth and short but grew heavier for the winter. The bulls were probably black with a white stripe down their backs, and they had a clump of curly white fur between their eyes.

Above: *Some cattle have a white stripe down their backs like the aurochs had.*

Above: *Types of Brahman cattle are raised in tropical countries like Costa Rica because they can tolerate the heat.*

The calves were red, and the cows were probably also reddish in color. Cave paintings of light-colored aurochsen, made by unknown artists 15,000 years ago, show some individuals that may have had a light saddle-shaped marking on their backs.

Aurochsen once lived in most parts of the Northern Hemisphere except North America. They were comfortable in open meadows but probably preferred living in forests. Overhunting by humans seems to be the main reason for their disappearance from the wild. Some scientists believe that three separate types were domesticated, since modern cattle show so much variety. The most common aurochs had long horns and a short forehead. Another variety had shorter horns with a longer forehead. The most distinctive kind probably lived wild in India and led to the modern zebu.

TAMING WILD CATTLE

During the 1930s and 1950s, zookeepers in Germany tried to recreate the aurochs by **crossbreeding** different kinds of cattle. They chose cows and bulls with traits like size, color, and horn shape similar to descriptions of the aurochs. They bred these cows and bulls, then selected the offspring that most resembled aurochsen and bred them together. Generations of careful breeding resulted in animals similar to the aurochs. Despite their large size, the resulting animals were very agile. They not only looked like aurochsen, they behaved like wild animals, too. They were shy around humans but could also be fierce. This fits with historical accounts, for Caesar wrote in 54 B.C. about the fierceness of the aurochs.

How and why would humans tame such a large and dangerous beast? Cattle were probably first domesticated in the Middle East about 9,000 years ago. By that time, people had already domesticated goats and sheep—animals of more manageable size and temperament. Perhaps the aurochs was

The Longhorn is an old breed with especially long, graceful horns.

These gaur are in the San Diego Wild Animal Park.

changed almost accidentally, in much the same way as an Asian relative called the mithan (also called the gayal) was domesticated. By looking at how mithan are treated today, we can imagine how they developed gradually from the gaur (GOW-er), a wild species of cattle that lives in the wooded hills of India. The mithan is smaller and gentler than the gaur. Its horns are differently shaped, and its face is flatter.

Mithan are allowed to roam freely through the woods but may also come into the villages at night for protection. The villagers put out salt to attract the mithan and keep them near. The animals are only disturbed when they are needed. They are not milked and are not normally killed for their meat. Instead, they are used only in trading and for animal sacrifices. Among some tribes, mithan are a measure of wealth. When one is sacrificed, the meat is eaten and the hide is used to make bags or to sit on. Occasions for sacrifice may include healing ceremonies for a very sick person or offerings to the spirit of someone who has died.

We can see how a large, fierce species could change gradually into a smaller, more gentle creature when treated like the mithan is today. The most nervous and shy animals would be likely to stay away from the villages. The calmer, gentler ones would come to lick the salt. This difference in behavior would result in separating the wilder animals, who would stay in the forest, from the more tamable ones, who would remain near the villages. Traits like calmness are at least partially inherited, so when the tamer animals bred together, their calves were likely to be like them. Over many generations, such breeding could result in a gentle domesticated race of animals that associated comfortably with humans.

The reduction in size of the domesticated animals can be explained another way. The largest, most magnificent bulls were selected for sacrifice. They would therefore breed less than the smaller bulls. Over time, since the larger animals bred less, the entire race would become smaller. The combination of size reduction and increased calmness resulted in a new kind of animal that has adapted to living with humans.

Scotch Highland cattle have changed little over hundreds of years. Some people believe they are more like the aurochs than most other breeds.

Calves born in late winter sometimes have a hard time if there is a blizzard. This one is doing just fine, with only a little snow on the ground.

Chapter 2

Cattle and People

L ike the mithan today, cattle were most likely used as ritual animals during the earliest days of their domestication. Thousands of years ago, religious sects that focused on cattle existed throughout the Mediterranean area. Cattle horns at a prehistoric settlement in what is now Turkey were found with fertility symbols and with small human figurines.

The ancient Egyptians admired a special type of black cattle with white markings called Apis cattle. An Apis bull had a pale saddle-shaped marking on his back, a white diamond on his forehead, and a spot on his tongue. Apis bulls with the proper markings were considered sacred. The Apis sect lasted for about a thousand years. Whenever one of the special bulls died, he was mummified and ceremonially buried in an underground rock tomb.

Opposite: *This calf finds human habitation worth investigating.*

Right: *Young Minoan athletes risked their lives somersaulting from the backs of bulls.*

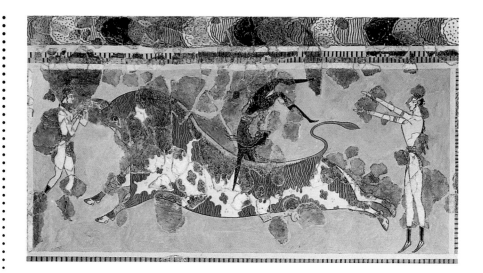

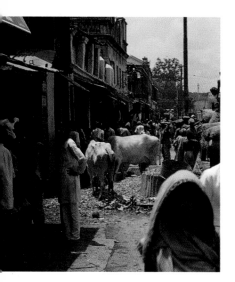

Above: *Sacred cattle roam the streets in India.*

During the Minoan times (about 2000 to 1600 B.C.) on the Mediterranean island of Crete, cattle were also considered sacred. Religious buildings were adorned with symbolic horns, and athletic young men and women played a life-and-death game vaulting from the backs of bulls.

Today, cattle are sacred animals in the Hindu religion and receive special treatment in Hindu countries. In India they are allowed to roam freely, even on city streets. In most of that country, as well as in some other Hindu countries, harming cattle is strictly against the law. Cattle can be milked and used for labor, however. But even after they become too old to work, laws require that they be cared for. India provides special nursing homes for old cows and bulls.

FROM THE SACRED TO THE PRACTICAL

At some time during the early association of cattle with humans, people began to use these animals for more than ritual purposes. Drawings on Egyptian tombs indicate that by about 5,000 years ago, cattle in Egypt were used for pulling plows and trampling grain to free the kernels from the husks. By 1900 B.C., the Egyptians had already bred distinctive cattle, such as a hornless, spotted breed and one with impressive lyre-shaped horns.

Cows and bulls have not usually been used as work animals; cows are too valuable for producing calves and milk, and bulls are too temperamental. But if a male's sex organs, the testicles, are removed when he is a young calf, the animal grows up to be much more even-tempered than a bull; he is called a **steer** or an **ox**. Steers are raised for meat, oxen are raised for labor and can be any breed. Unlike bulls, steers and oxen don't fight when they are kept together in corrals. Oxen have been used to pull plows, carts, and wagons for thousands of years. Many of the pioneers who settled the American West used oxen to pull their covered wagons.

Below: *In late spring, cattle are rounded up. The calves are branded, and the male calves' testicles are removed.*

Left: *This impressive ox is an Ayrshire, which is a dairy breed.*

Cows were probably first milked in Egypt and Mesopotamia around 6,000 years ago. The practice of milking was taken up in other areas as well, such as in northern Europe, where cheese making became important. Once milk is made into cheese, it becomes a very nourishing, concentrated food that can be stored in a cool place for long periods of time, providing an important food source for the long winter months.

CATTLE AS FOOD

In at least some religious rites, cattle were eaten after they were sacrificed, so humans have been eating beef for a long time. No one knows when the raising of cattle specifically for food began, however. Some Egyptian artwork shows cattle being force-fed to make them fatter, presumably for use as food.

Today, there are several breeds of cattle raised specifically for meat, and others that are raised specifically for milk. A milking breed puts most of the energy it gets from food into making milk. Its body looks somewhat bony and thin, even when it is healthy. A meat breed, on the other hand, produces just enough milk to feed its young. Most of its energy goes into the muscles that will be meat after the animal is slaughtered. The bulls of some meat breeds have so much muscle that they weigh in at almost 2 tons.

Opposite (top): *These dairy cattle look bony, but they are healthy.*

Opposite (bottom): *People have been milking cows for thousands of years.*

Left: *Beef cattle are powerfully muscled.*

Chapter 3

The Closest
Cattle Relatives

Above: *A yak calf*

Along with cattle, *Bos taurus*, scientists include four more species in the genus *Bos*: the yak, gaur, banteng, and kouprey. They are cattle's closest relatives. All of them have large, heavy bodies and strong legs. Both males and females have horns.

THE YAK

Yaks *(Bos grunniens)* live as both wild and domesticated animals at high altitudes in central Asia. Wild yaks are much larger than domesticated ones and are usually dark brown. Domesticated yaks have a variety of colors. They are also sometimes crossbred with domesticated cattle. Yaks have long, heavy coats of hair that help keep them warm in their rugged, cold habitat. The Tibetan people use their yaks as pack animals and riding mounts as well as a source for milk.

Opposite: *Domesticated yaks can have a variety of coat colors.*

Once a year, the animals' long coat is shorn. Each yak provides about 6.5 pounds of coarse wool, which is used to make blankets and clothing.

THE GAUR

The gaur, from which the mithan developed, is scientifically named *Bos gaurus*. It lives in the forests and meadows of the hilly regions of Burma, Malaysia, and India. It feeds on grass and plant shoots, mostly at night. The gaur is a typical bovid—groups of 2 to 40 cows and calves travel together, usually with no more than a single mature bull. Most bulls live either alone or in small groups with other bulls. During the breeding season, bulls travel in search of cows and may spar with one another but don't seem to get into serious fights.

The gaur, Bos gaurus, *is a typical bovid.*

THE BANTENG

The banteng *(Bos javanicus)* shares some areas with the gaur, but its range extends farther south, onto the islands of

Borneo and Java. Its social life is similar to the gaur. It lives in drier, more open areas, but it will retreat into the forest to escape enemies. Before World War II, banteng in Thailand spent the mornings and afternoons grazing on the open meadows, resting in the forest during the heat of the day. After the war, however, the animals were hunted so much that they are now likely to come out only at night, spending the daylight hours in the dense forests where they are safe from hunters. None of the 90 different foods they eat is found in undisturbed forests, so banteng can only survive in areas where people have cut down parts of the forest, creating clearings where the animals can feed.

On the islands of Java and Bali, the banteng has been domesticated and is used for milk and meat, as well as for labor. Domesticated banteng can thrive under very hot and humid conditions, which stress cattle. They can stay in good condition on poor pastureland. Their tough hides with short hair help them resist ticks and the diseases ticks carry. Since 1913, the government of Indonesia has forbidden crossbreeding of these useful animals with cattle for fear the banteng will lose its special traits.

Banteng look very much like domesticated cattle.

THE KOUPREY

The kouprey *(Bos sauveli)* is a very rare wild bovid that lives in the hills of Indochina, where war has been destroying them and their home areas for more than 50 years. Koupreys have a very long dewlap of loose skin under their necks. In old bulls, the dewlap almost touches the ground. Biologists are interested in the kouprey, since it may be resistant to some of the diseases that kill cattle. They hope that crossbreeding kouprey with cattle might bring those resistances into cattle. But the kouprey is so rare that it could become extinct before crossbreeding can even be tried.

Chapter 4

Cattle and Bison through the Year

Above: *A lone bison bull in Yellowstone National Park*

Since the aurochs died out over 300 years ago, we know little about its behavior. But we can learn something of why cattle behave the way they do by looking at a familiar wild relative, the American bison—also called the buffalo. Bison are closely enough related to cattle that the two species can interbreed, and both thrive on open grasslands. Bison were once threatened with extinction, but thousands now live on public and private lands across North America.

BISON SOCIAL LIFE

Most of the year, bison cows, calves, and young bulls live in groups of anywhere from 12 to 200 individuals. A dominant cow leads the group from place to place. The adult bulls keep to themselves, either in small groups or alone.

Opposite: *You can see how much bigger a bison bull is than a bison cow.*

29

Right: *The bulls fighting in the background are stirring up dust. The other bison don't seem to take much notice.*

Above: *The bull has thick, curly hair on his forehead to cushion the blows of fighting.*

When breeding season comes in late summer, things change. The smaller groups merge into larger ones, and bulls challenge one another for the right to breed with the cows. If neither bull backs down during a challenge between two bulls, a fight may result. The bulls bang their heads together, putting the entire force of their huge, 1-ton bodies behind the clash. The thick, curly fur on each bull's forehead helps soften the blow. Usually, one animal gives up within seconds or minutes. Chances are that the battles of aurochsen were also quite intense, like those of bison, given the tuft of curly fur they had on their foreheads.

The bulls of domesticated cattle also butt heads when they fight one another, but their battles aren't as spectacular as those of the bison. They can, however, fight hard enough to cause a serious injury, such as a broken leg.

Cattle have a social system similar to that of bison. One bull is dominant over the others in a pasture and manages to do most of the mating, just as with bison. Among the cows of both species there is a **dominance hierarchy**. This means that each cow has her place in the herd. One is "top cow." If she wants to graze in a particular place or drink from a puddle, the other cows move aside. The second-ranking cow will give in to Number One, but all the others let Number Two have her way. The third-ranking cow defers to One and Two, and so forth through the herd. There may be a few exceptions to this hierarchy, but the system generally works this way. In both species, the calves end up with a ranking similar to that of their mothers; calves of top-ranking cows also rank high, while those of cows at the bottom are also at the bottom.

The cows in a pasture get to know one another well. When new cows are added, it takes time before they become a real part of the herd. They need to work out their relationships with the other cows, which can cause problems for a rancher when it's time to drive the cattle together into a new pasture.

In both bison (above) and cattle (below), the calf has a similar social status as its mother.

Bison mothers are very protective of their calves; so are domesticated cattle.

MOTHERS AND CALVES

Bison calves are born in the springtime, mostly in May. The mother bison licks her calf to fluff up its fur and help it dry out. In the first few minutes after birth, the calf and cow learn to recognize one another by smell and by the sound of each other's voices. That way, they can always find one another if they get separated.

The calf can get on its feet within minutes of being born. Very quickly, it finds the mother's udder and begins to nurse. The cow is very protective of her youngster, especially at first. All the bison cows eventually share in taking care of the calves. Sometimes, one "baby-sitter" will watch over the young animals while the other mothers graze.

The life of cattle mothers and calves is very similar to that of bison. This is not surprising since successful raising of the young is just as important to a domesticated animal as it is to a wild one. Like bison calves, young cattle are on their feet soon after birth. They learn quickly to recognize their mothers, and their mothers learn to recognize them. They soon find the vital udder from which they can drink warm, nourishing milk. Domestic cows are also very protective of their young, chasing off coyotes and other potential enemies. And like bison, cows take turns baby-sitting the calves.

While bison breed only in late summer, cattle can mate at any time of the year. Both species give birth about nine-and-a-half months after mating. Most ranchers who raise beef cattle breed their cows so that the calves will be born sometime between February and April. The earlier they are born, the sooner they can be sent to market.

A calf being born

The mother licks her calf as soon as it's born.

The calf struggles to stand up within a few minutes of birth.

Left: *Soon, the calf is looking for its mother's milk.*

Right: *Nowadays, cows are mostly milked by machine.*

Above: *Dairy cows are often fed while they are being milked to keep them contented.*

BISON AND DAIRY CATTLE DIFFER

There are big differences between bison and dairy cattle, however. In the first place, unlike bison, dairy cattle are bred to produce large amounts of milk, much more than a calf would need. Secondly, bison milk is much richer—it has more fat—than cow's milk. The most popular breed of dairy cattle, the black-and-white Holstein, has been bred to produce enormous quantities of milk with little fat.

Another difference lies in the willingness of the animals to be milked. Normally, a wild animal will only let its own baby nurse. But generations of breeding have resulted in cows that will allow themselves to be milked by people and machines. Usually, the dairy cow's calf is taken away shortly after birth and fed separately, for the convenience of the farmer.

Milking can still be tricky, however. The cows become used to their normal routine, and it's important that the routine go smoothly or they can become upset and not let their milk down. Farmers have ways of helping the cows feel relaxed. For example, some play music in the milking barn. Feeding the cows at milking time also helps make them comfortable.

CATTLE THROUGH THE YEAR

Wild animals can take care of themselves. But domesticated animals often need human help at some points in their lives. For instance, bison can make it through the toughest winter on their own. They use their huge heads to push aside the snow so they can get at the grass underneath. But cattle don't know how to find grass under the snow. They must be fed hay every day during the wintertime in areas where it snows.

Bison cows don't usually mate until they are two years old. But cattle can breed at one year of age, and ranchers are eager to get their young cows, called **heifers**, reproducing as soon as possible. A bred heifer is about two when her calf is born. But since a two-year-old cow isn't full grown, she can have trouble giving birth if the calf is large. For this reason, ranchers often have to help their young cows give birth. To make it easier, they may use a bull of a smaller breed to mate with their first-year heifers.

Above: *Longhorn bulls are often bred with young cows.*

Above: *Bison can use their huge heads, powered by their strong shoulder muscles, to push away snow to get to food.*

Left: *Cattle must be fed every day during the wintertime.*

Above: *This Brown Swiss cow has a pretty face.*

Chapter 5

Bovines in Today's World

Cattle are among the most valuable animals in the world. No one knows just how many there are, but estimates put the number over one billion. Cattle can live in very dry areas, like the Nevada deserts, as long as there is water to drink. They can be left on their own for months at a time, then rounded up before winter and fed during the coldest months. Large numbers of cattle graze on public lands, such as national forests. Ranchers pay a small fee for each animal put out to graze. Some people think too many cattle are allowed on certain lands, and the cattle are damaging the range by killing native grasses.

Opposite: *At the end of summer, range cattle are rounded up and taken to where they can be fed during the winter.*

Many breeds of cattle are becoming rare. In the United States today, most of the dairy cattle belong to just one breed, the Holstein-Friesan, usually called simply the Holstein. Smaller numbers of four other breeds—Ayrshire, Guernsey, Jersey, and Brown Swiss—are also parts of some dairy herds. The same is true with beef cattle—most of our beef comes from only a few breeds of cattle, such as the Angus and the Hereford.

Each breed has traits that make it special. Breeds that are becoming rare may have traits such as disease resistance that could become very important in the future. Fortunately, some people are working hard to keep these less popular animals from disappearing completely.

These are Angus cattle. The calf's father, however, was probably a Charolais because its coat is a smokey gray.

Left: *Cattle in a feedlot have little space.*

Above: *Charolais is a French cattle breed that is becoming more popular in the United States.*

ARE CATTLE TREATED HUMANELY?

Some people are concerned about how cattle are treated. Beef cattle are generally allowed to graze on the pasture during the summer months. But when the steers are sold by the rancher, they are usually sent to enclosures called feedlots. In feedlots, animals are fed mostly grains such as corn, a concentrated food that helps them put on weight rapidly. Feedlots are often highly mechanized so that one person can feed as many as 10,000 cattle a day. A typical feedlot allows only 75 square feet per animal, so the cattle can't move about very much. The crowded cattle have no grass to nibble or lie on. Instead, their manure is made into a big pile where they can lie down. Cattle are kept in feedlots for three to four months before going to market.

When the cattle are ready for slaughter, they are sent to the slaughterhouse, where workers stun them, sometimes with an electric gun, before they are killed. Many people are concerned about the animals being crowded together and restrained for a long time before their deaths.

The most serious complaint about cruelty to cattle is the way veal calves are usually raised. The calves are taken from their mothers at or shortly after birth and put into individual stalls lined up row upon row in a barn. Each stall is only 2 feet wide and 4.5 feet long. The floor is made of slats, making footing difficult. The calves can barely move and never get a chance to romp and play together in the sunshine. Although calves naturally begin nibbling on grass at a very young age, veal calves are given no grass or hay, only a liquid food much higher in fat content than milk. The calf food lacks iron, a mineral that gives meat its red color. This makes the calves **anemic** and unwell. They are given **antibiotics** to keep them from getting seriously ill.

Veal growers claim that people want to eat veal that is pale in color rather than reddish, and that veal from calves allowed to move about isn't as mild and tender. But other people say this isn't so. They raise veal humanely, either by letting the calves stay with their mothers and feed on their milk, or by keeping several calves together in corrals where they can play together and have hay to eat. Humanely raised veal, these veal growers say, tastes just as good as the pale kind.

Opposite: *Cows, whether they are cattle (top) or bison (bottom) lick their calves, even when they have become quite large.*

Below: *Veal calves should be allowed to live outdoors with other calves, like these young dairy cattle.*

Dairy cows know when it's milking time. Unfortunately, family farms, like this one, are being replaced by huge operations in which the cows are treated like numbers rather than living beings.

CONCERNS ABOUT DAIRY CATTLE

People worry about dairy cattle, too. Dairies keep getting bigger, with less attention being paid to the individual cows. Instead of names, the cows have numbers. Their calves are taken away at birth, so the cows never get a chance to behave like normal mothers; they have become milk-producing machines. In 1950, a dairy cow gave an average of 618 gallons of milk each year. Now the average is up to 1,703 gallons.

A major concern now about dairy cows is the proposed use of the **hormone** BGH. Some people want to give BGH to cows so they will produce even more milk than they already do. As it is, cows are often expected to give more milk than is healthy for them. They easily become sick and are given drugs. Some of these drugs are dangerous to humans, yet they can show up in the milk. Giving cows BGH would only stress them more, increasing the chances of illness. As it is, there are too many dairy cattle in the United States, and the government buys the excess milk.

IS BEEF A HEALTHY FOOD?

Many people wonder whether beef is a healthy food. They worry about the hormones and antibiotics given to the animals to make them grow faster. Beef producers say that these chemicals are all gone by the time the animals are slaughtered, but some people aren't sure that's true.

People also worry about the safety of milk and milk products. Some claim that dangerous chemicals such as pesticides, which may have been sprayed on the grains cattle eat, become concentrated in food like cheese.

Years ago, people liked to eat beef with lots of fat in it. A well-marbled steak—one with many streaks of white fat—was considered a special treat. Now we know that it's unhealthy for us to eat too much animal fat. Beef growers are raising animals that produce leaner beef with less marbling, butchers are trimming more and more fat from the meat they sell, and most stores now sell extra-lean ground beef. Eating beef every day might not be a good idea, but lean beef can be included safely as part of a varied diet.

Grass-fed cattle, like these, produce tasty, lean meat.

The beefalo is a hardy cross between cattle and bison that produces delicious meat that is low in fat.

In addition to extra-lean beef, bison meat, called buffalo, shows up in some supermarkets. It is leaner than beef. The desire for lean meat has also led to the increasing popularity for beefalo, a cross between cattle and bison. The beefalo can survive harsher conditions and produces leaner meat than cattle.

THE FATE OF THE WILD

Like many other wild animals, the close relatives of cattle are losing out in today's crowded world. Each of the four species is in danger of extinction. The kouprey is the rarest of all. Southeast Asian countries are cooperating to try to study and save this potentially valuable animal.

The kouprey isn't the only close relative that has value for crossbreeding with cattle. In Indonesia, Madura cattle, a cross between banteng and zebu, are used mostly for racing; they can run as fast as horses. But besides their value as racers, these cattle produce very tender beef, and the leather from their hides is especially soft. They grow faster than banteng and do well with poor nutrition, even when it is very hot. Americans have also crossed banteng and cattle with some success. In Texas, a one-eighth banteng, seven-eighths

Charolais cross shows promise as a beef breed for warm, humid climates.

The wild relatives of cattle have been overhunted too, and all are losing their homes to the growing human population of Asia. In addition, the gaur is susceptible to the diseases of domesticated cattle, and the banteng interbreeds with cattle, threatening its own pure, wild strain. The wild yak is officially protected in China but is still hunted. At least the yak and the banteng also exist as domesticated animals, and the gaur carries on in its modified, domesticated form—the mithan. But wild animals have their own traits that make them different from domesticated ones. The world would be a less interesting place if these magnificent animals were to disappear from the planet. Their disappearance could also result in the loss of important **genetic** traits that could be bred into cattle.

The domestication of cattle was an important step for civilization. Their sheer power allowed huge loads to be taken from place to place. Domesticating cattle may have led to the crucial invention that made transportation easy—the wheel. And the versatility of cattle, providing power, meat, milk, fertilizer, and leather, cannot be matched by any other domesticated animal. For these reasons, the partnership between humans and cattle has special significance to civilization.

Humane Farming
Organizations

For more information on where you can find chemically free and humanely raised food, contact the Humane Farming Association and the Food Animal Concerns Trust.

The Humane Farming Association (HFA) campaigns to protect consumers from the dangerous misuse of chemicals in food production, and to eliminate the severe and senseless suffering to which farm animals are subjected. For more information, please write or call HFA.

Humane Farming Association
1550 California Street
San Francisco, California 94109
415-771-CALF

The Food Animal Concerns Trust is concerned with the way farm animals are treated and encourages research into humane ways of raising livestock. If you would like to know more about how cattle and poultry are raised, you can write to Food Animal Concerns Trust (FACT).

Food Animal Concerns Trust
P.O. Box 14599
Chicago, Illinois 60614

METRIC CONVERSION CHART		
WHEN YOU KNOW:	MULTIPLY BY:	TO FIND:
feet	30.48	centimeters
square feet	.09	square meters
pounds	.454	kilograms
gallons	3.787	liters

Glossary

anemic: deficient in iron and lacking vitality

antibiotics: a medicine that can cure or inhibit certain diseases

cellulose: a chemical that makes up the major part of plant leaves and stems and is difficult to digest

crossbreeding: mating two individuals of different breeds, varieties, or species

domesticate: to shape a species of animal over time to live with and assist humans

dominance hierarchy *(HI-er-ark-ee)***:** a social structure that is based on a pecking order in which individual members back down or stand up to one another, depending on their established rank

extinct: when all the members of a species have died

genetic: referring to the traits an organism inherits from its parents

heifers: young cows, especially ones that have not yet given birth to calves

hormone: a substance produced by glands in the body that stimulates organs in particular ways. Hormones can also be made in the laboratory.

ox: a domesticated bull raised for labor whose testicles have been removed

ruminants: animals that have a three- or four-chambered stomach and rechew their food in the form of cuds

steer: a domesticated bull raised for meat whose testicles have been removed

tamed: to have accustomed an individual animal to the presence of humans

Index

Pages listed in **bold** type refer to photographs.